❦ History *of* Britain ❦
Tudor Palaces
and Other Great Houses

Andrew Langley

Illustrated by Mark Bergin and James Field

HISTORY OF BRITAIN – TUDOR PALACES AND OTHER GREAT HOUSES
was produced for Heinemann Children's Reference
by Lionheart Books, London.

Editors: Lionel Bender and Peter MacDonald
Designer: Ben White
Design Assistant: Michael Weintroub
Picture Researcher: Jennie Karrach
Media Conversion and Typesetting: Peter MacDonald
Educational Consultant: Jane Shuter
Editorial Advisors: Andrew Farrow, Paul Shuter

Production Controller: Lorraine Stebbing
Editorial Director: David Riley

First published in Great Britain in 1997 by
Heinemann Educational Publishers, a division of Reed
Educational and Professional Publishing Limited,
Halley Court, Jordan Hill, Oxford OX2 8EJ.

MADRID ATHENS
FLORENCE PRAGUE WARSAW
PORTSMOUTH NH CHICAGO SAO PAULO MEXICO
SINGAPORE TOKYO MELBOURNE AUCKLAND
IBADAN GABORONE JOHANNESBURG KAMPALA NAIROBI

ISBN 0431 057133 Hb   ISBN 0431 057176 Pb

British Library Cataloguing-in-Publication Data.
A catalogue record for this book is available
from the British Library.

Printed in Italy

Acknowledgements
Picture credits
t = top, b = bottom, c = centre, l = left, r = right.
Pages: 5t: Hatfield House, Herts. 5b: © Crown Copyright, Historic Royal
Palaces. 6t: Ashmolean Museum, Oxford. 6b: Fitzwilliam Museum,
University of Cambridge/Bridgeman Art Library, London. 8t: Courtesy of
the Trustees of the Victoria and Albert Museum, London. 9t: Buccleuch
Recreational Enterprises Ltd., Scotland. 10tr: Automobile Association
Photo Library. 11tl: Kentwell Hall, Long Melford, Suffolk. 11tr: National
Trust Photographic Library. 12-13t, 13tr: Fotomas Index. 14-15t:
Collection of the Earl of Derby, Suffolk/Bridgeman Art Library, London.
15c: © Museum of London. 15cl: Fotomas Index. 15br: National Trust
Photographic Library. 16br: Bodleian Library, Oxford. 17t: Courtesy of
the Trustees of the Victoria and Albert Museum, London. 17b: The Royal
Collection Enterprises/© Her Majesty the Queen. 18tl: Fotomas Index.
18tr, 19tr: Museum of London. 19c: English Life Publications Limited,
Derby. 20b: Fotomas Index. 20c: By Courtesy of the Trustees of the
British Museum, London (Sloane 1832 f.7.v), 21b: Fotomas Index. 22bl:
Automobile Assocation Photo Library. 22cr: Courtesy of the National
Portrait Gallery, London (NPG710).

Artwork credits
All artwork by Mark Bergin, except for map on page 23 by Stefan
Chabluk.
Cover: Main illustration by Mark Bergin. Photo: Fotomas Index.

PLACES TO VISIT

Here are some great Tudor houses which still stand today.
Your local Tourist Office will be able to tell you about other
places in your area.

Buckland Abbey, Devon. Tudor explorer Francis Drake's
home. Good for exhibits of Tudor daily life.

Burghley House, Lincolnshire. Built in 1589 by Queen
Elizabeth I's chief advisor, this has been the home of the
Cecil family ever since.

Castle Fraser, Aberdeenshire. The Scots built traditional
castles like this, even in Tudor times.

Compton Wynyates, Warwickshire. A beautiful early Tudor
house, with battlements and the remains of a moat.

Hampton Court Palace, London. Built by Sir Thomas
Wolsey, this huge palace was taken over by Henry VIII.

Hardwick Hall, Derbyshire. A dazzling Tudor house full of
huge windows, and displaying lots of Tudor furniture and
tapestry.

Hever Castle, Kent. Moated home of the family of Anne
Boleyn, one of Henry VIII's wives.

Holyrood Palace, Edinburgh. The palace where Mary, Queen
of Scots, lived as ruler and, later, as prisoner.

Kenilworth Castle, Warwickshire. The home of Queen
Elizabeth I's close admirer, Robert Dudley. The queen made
three visits to the house.

Kentwell Hall and Melford Hall, Long Melford, Suffolk. Two
Tudor manor houses with lawns and gardens. Kentwell
holds re-creations of Tudor life.

Knole, Kent. This huge, rambling Tudor house was once a
royal palace. It is surrounded by a vast deer park.

Little Moreton Hall, Cheshire. A fine example of 'half-
timbered' (black and white) Tudor houses.

Longleat House, Wiltshire. The first of the grand, ornate
Elizabethan houses.

Montacute House, Somerset. This magnificent Elizabethan
house has a display of Elizabethan portraits from the
National Portrait Gallery.

National Portrait Gallery, London. Many paintings of Tudor
personalities.

Penshurst Place, Kent. Among many other treasures, this
site boasts a Tudor Garden.

Wollaton Hall, Nottinghamshire. The most fantastic of all the
'prodigy' Tudor houses.

The Vyne, Hampshire. A brickwork house built in Henry VIII's
reign.

INTRODUCTION

During medieval times in Britain there were often civil wars and rebellions. Noblemen and barons lived in strongholds, behind moats and gates and grim castle walls. Then in 1485 Henry VII became the first Tudor king. He brought lasting peace, and the nobles no longer had to protect themselves. Some converted their castles into comfortable homes. Others built huge new houses instead. So began a great age of English building.

In 1534, Henry VIII closed down many monasteries and abbeys and sold or gave away their land to courtiers and other powerful people. The new owners wanted their homes to be the grandest and most richly decorated of all, in order to show how important they were.

CONTENTS

BUILDING A PALACE

"Every man almost is a builder," wrote an English traveller in 1577, **"and will not be quiet till he have pulled down the old house and set up a new."** During the reigns of Henry VIII and Elizabeth I, more than 50 palaces and great houses were built.

Many old houses and church buildings were pulled down to make room for the new houses and manors. Henry VIII had a whole village in Surrey flattened in 1538 so that he could build Nonsuch Palace.

Most medieval houses had been made of timber and plaster. But the new Tudor builders usually preferred brick or stone. These materials were stronger and longer lasting, and they could be moulded or carved into ornate shapes.

▽ **Craftsmen working on the elaborate roof of Burghley House** in Lincolnshire in the 1570s. A carpenter cuts timbers that will support the lead roof-covering.

▽ **The master craftsman prepares his plans for Burghley House.** Lord Burghley, Elizabeth I's chief minister, began to build this great house in 1564.

△ **The mason** cut and shaped stone using saw, hammer and chisel.

△ **The carpenter** made wooden windows, doors and staircases.

▽ **The blacksmith** beat and bent metal to make nails and fences.

▽ **The bricklayer** built up brick walls held together with mortar.

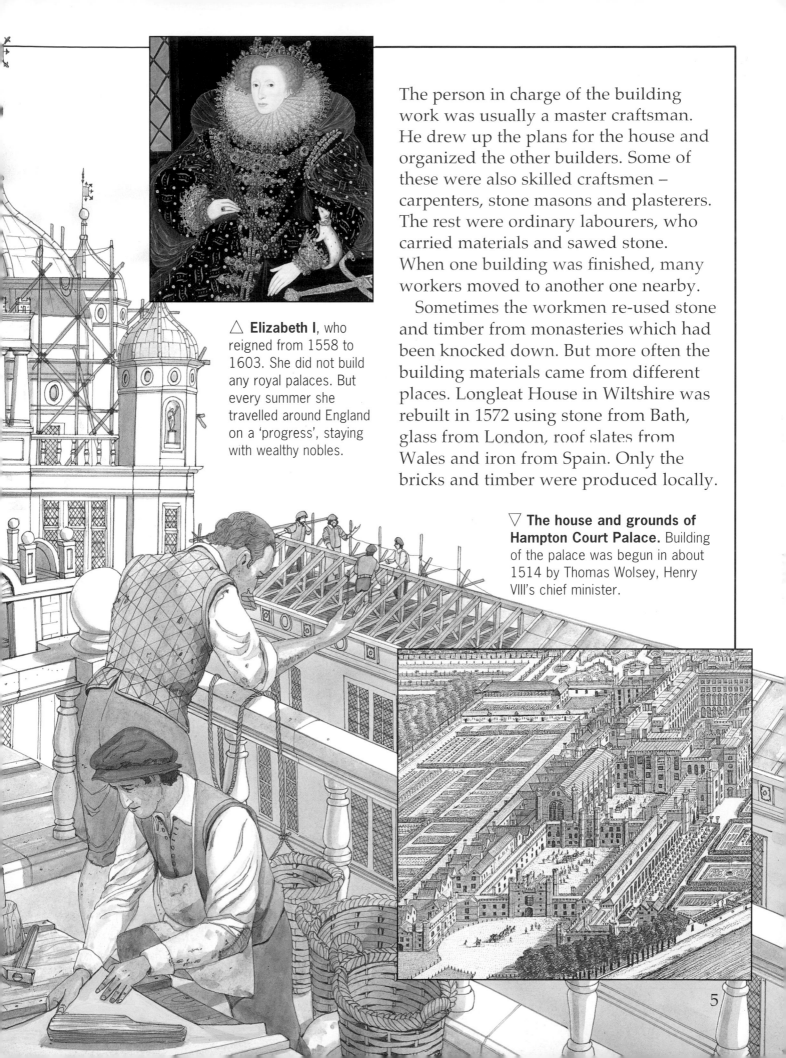

△ **Elizabeth I**, who reigned from 1558 to 1603. She did not build any royal palaces. But every summer she travelled around England on a 'progress', staying with wealthy nobles.

The person in charge of the building work was usually a master craftsman. He drew up the plans for the house and organized the other builders. Some of these were also skilled craftsmen – carpenters, stone masons and plasterers. The rest were ordinary labourers, who carried materials and sawed stone. When one building was finished, many workers moved to another one nearby.

Sometimes the workmen re-used stone and timber from monasteries which had been knocked down. But more often the building materials came from different places. Longleat House in Wiltshire was rebuilt in 1572 using stone from Bath, glass from London, roof slates from Wales and iron from Spain. Only the bricks and timber were produced locally.

▽ **The house and grounds of Hampton Court Palace.** Building of the palace was begun in about 1514 by Thomas Wolsey, Henry VIII's chief minister.

INSIDE AND OUT

The grand palaces of Elizabeth I's reign have been called 'prodigy' houses (a prodigy is something that is marvellous or wonderful). They were meant to look splendid, unlike the grim castles of medieval times. Owners chose to build them in places where they could be seen from far away.

▽**Richmond Palace by the River Thames in Surrey.** It was finished in 1501 by craftsmen hired by Henry VII. This early Tudor house still looks like a castle, with tall towers, turrets and battlements.

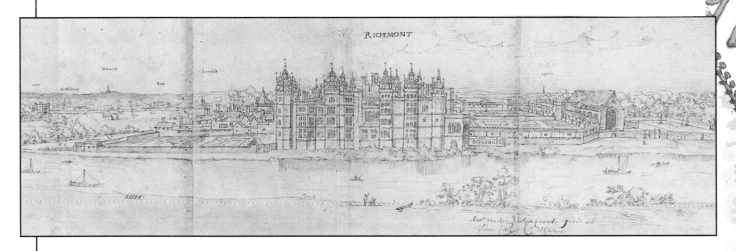

A prodigy house such as Longleat had a regular shape, with each side matching the one opposite. At the centre of the front was the grand entrance. Some houses were built around a courtyard. Others, such as Hardwick Hall, were simple box shapes. The outer walls were decorated with columns and other carved stonework. Towers and ornate chimneys rose above the line of the roof.

The most marvellous features of these houses were the windows. By the 1550s, glass had become quite cheap. Prodigy houses had a lot of very large windows. Hardwick Hall had so many that people said it was "more glass than wall". By day, thousands of tiny panes glittered in the sun. At night, the light from inside the house made it glow like a lantern.

Inside, these houses were brighter and more splendid than any castle. The stone walls were no longer left bare, but were covered with timber panels or colourful tapestries. Instead of stone spiral steps, there were open staircases of wood, with richly carved banisters and posts. Ceilings were timber-panelled or painted.

▽ **Nonsuch Palace** at the time of James I, c. 1620.

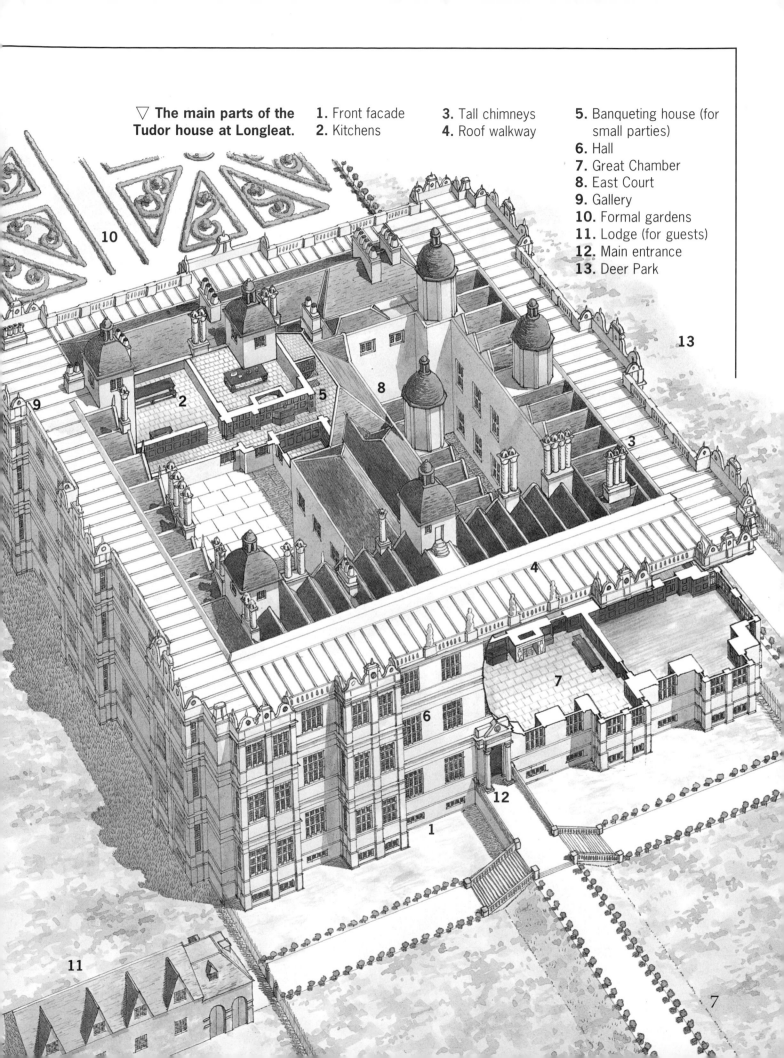

▽ **The main parts of the Tudor house at Longleat.**

1. Front facade
2. Kitchens
3. Tall chimneys
4. Roof walkway
5. Banqueting house (for small parties)
6. Hall
7. Great Chamber
8. East Court
9. Gallery
10. Formal gardens
11. Lodge (for guests)
12. Main entrance
13. Deer Park

NOBLEMAN AND HOUSEHOLD

The owner of a great house might spend the winter in London at the monarch's court. But London in summer was an unhealthy place. The heat and filth increased the risk of catching diseases such as the plague. Summers were spent in the country.

◁ **A miniature (tiny portrait) of a little girl** aged five holding a carnation flower. Wealthy parents treated their children as small adults. The miniature was painted by Isaac Oliver in 1590. Oliver was a student of artist Nicholas Hilliard, who was the court painter to Elizabeth I and James I.

▽ **Noblemen's children** were dressed like their parents in elaborate clothes, and were expected to behave as grown-ups. Some nobles sent their children to a great house to be looked after and to learn how to behave. The children became part of the household, which was made up of the owner, his family, relatives who came to stay, and his servants.

▷ **A nobleman with his wife and children** and with the steward (manager) of his household, who wears a gold chain of office. The nobleman was the most powerful person in the area. His 'manor', or lands, might include villages and the surrounding farmland. The nobleman ran his manor as a business, which brought him money, food and materials. The people who lived in his villages or farmed his land had to pay him rent. This might be cash, or food and firewood. They also had to pay if they wanted their corn ground in the nobleman's mill. His wife organized the household and servants.

The nobleman's children lived in luxury and did not mix with other youngsters. When they were small, they played in the gardens or in the galleries upstairs. At the age of three or four they began taking lessons at home with a hired tutor. They learned Greek, Latin and French, as well as dancing and music.

◁ **A group of household gentlemen**, wearing the 'livery', or uniform, of their lord. Such clothes were often very colourful and costly, with gold chains and silk coats. They were a way of showing off the lord's wealth.

△ **A young lady from a noble family** at her dressing table. A nobleman was a powerful person who promised to serve the monarch. He usually supplied the monarch with soldiers in time of war and received grants of land in return.

The nobleman and his family spent their summers at the country house, hunting and entertaining. The house was run by the senior members of the household (servants), who were usually men from other powerful families. The most important gentleman was the steward, who organized the working of the land. The 'comptroller' (controller) was in charge of the money accounts.

The owners of great Tudor houses did not all come from noble families. Many people from humble beginnings became rich and powerful. Thomas Wolsey, a butcher's son, became Chancellor of England and built Hampton Court. John Thynne, who built Longleat, was once the steward of a duke. Hardwick Hall was built by Bess of Hardwick, the daughter of a poor country squire.

How the House Worked

Guests at a great Tudor house saw only the grandest areas. They came in through the hall and went up the staircase to the upper floors. After visiting a friend's new house in 1579, Lord Burghley wrote "I found no one thing of greater grace than your stately ascent (climb) from your hall to your great chamber".

The great chamber was the biggest and most important room in the house. Here the lord held feasts for his guests. The chamber was beautifully decorated, with tapestries or painted plaster on the walls and stained glass in the windows.

Leading off the great chamber was a much smaller room, the 'withdrawing chamber'. The owner retreated here to sit in private with his family and friends, leaving his other guests behind. Beyond it was the lord's bedchamber.

Guests who were not invited into the withdrawing room could wander in the gallery. At first, galleries were simply places where people could stroll under shelter if it was raining. Later, they were used more. They had moulded plaster ceilings, and paintings on the walls.

Below, on the ground floor, were the working areas – the kitchens, scullery and store rooms. There were outhouses for baking bread, brewing beer and making butter and cheese. Servants usually slept in attics at the very top of the house.

▷ (Above) **The gateway of Stanway House** in Gloucestershire.

▷ **Local 'gentlemen' and ladies who served the lord.**

▷ **The local villagers.** They worked the land, growing crops and cutting firewood to supply the kitchens.

△ **A cutaway view of a great Tudor house, its courtyard and gardens.** Nobles and their staff are arriving for a long stay at the house. Around the house lies the park, with a strong fence. Here the owner and his guests would hunt deer on horseback, or fly hawks to catch rabbits and birds.

△ **The front of Kentwell Hall,** in Suffolk.

▷ **The house servants came from families on the manor.**

△ **The Long Gallery at Packwood House** in Warwickshire. Tapestries hang on the walls under the wooden ceiling.

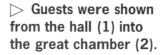

▷ **Guests were shown from the hall (1) into the great chamber (2).**

▷ **An owner rested in his withdrawing chamber (3).** Important guests were invited into this private room after a meal. The owner's personal servants slept here so that they could be called for quickly.

▷ **The nobleman and his wife in their bedchamber (4),** attended by their personal servants. The wife often had her own bedchamber, joined to her husband's by a passageway.

▷ **In many big houses, the owner had a private inner chamber (5).** There was also a grand apartment, bedchamber and private chamber for the king or queen, who might visit.

THE SERVANTS

Big houses needed numerous servants. In 1595, Lord Montague drew up a list of his staff. The list had 37 different jobs, many of which needed several people. They included "My Carver, The Yeomen of My Wardrobe, The Chief Cook, The Porter, The Grooms of the Great Chamber and The Scullery Man".

△ **Yeomen of the Wardrobe** had many duties, especially when there were guests. Lord Montague ordered his yeomen to "see the galleries and all lodgings reserved for strangers cleanly and sweetly kept, with herbs and flowers". They laid out bedding at night and removed it in the morning.

△ **Servers prepare the Great Chamber for a meal.** Those in charge of the lord's 'ewery' looked after the table linen and laid the cloths. After the meal, they served water in silver jugs called ewers, so that diners could wash their hands. Yeoman waiters carried food and drink to the tables.

△ **Two minstrels.** Most noblemen hired musicians to entertain the family and guests and to play the music that went with short plays called masques. These were performed in the Great Chamber after feasts. The most popular instruments were the lute, the viol (an early violin) and the trumpet.

There were three sorts of servants. First came the gentlemen, who were from noble families. Below them were the yeomen, who were the sons of farmers and landowners. Last were the grooms. These were usually peasants from the local villages. Female servants attended the ladies of the house or worked in places like the dairy or laundry.

Most servants worked in the house itself. They cleaned the rooms, lit fires, waited at table, looked after the master's clothes and welcomed guests. In the kitchens there were men in charge of cooking and beermaking. They tended the wine cellars, the buttery and store rooms. Stonemasons and carpenters kept the house in good repair.

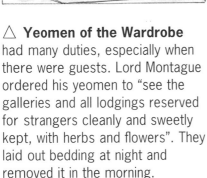

◁ **Farmworkers cut corn** and tie it up into bundles or sheaves. Most villagers still had to work in their lord's fields for a set number of days each year.

▷ **The blacksmith made nails**, tools and horseshoes for the big house and its estate.

△ **A Gentleman of the Horse**, part of the huge stable staff. Horses not only had to be fed, stabled, groomed and harnessed. Young horses were highly trained for long-distance travel or hunting. Disobedient horses might be punished horribly by having a hedgehog put under their tails.

△ **A servant cleans out the garderobe or privy.** This was the small room where buckets were used as toilets. The nobleman and important guests would have their own buckets.The content of the buckets were thrown on to the 'midden', or muckheap, which then went to the palace gardens.

△ **A servant making cheese in the buttery.** As much food as possible had to be preserved for the harsh winter months. Milk was turned into cheese, or into butter, which was packed in barrels. Meat was preserved by salting, or by being smoked (hung inside a chimney until it was dried out).

Outside, yet more servants tended the park and the farmland. Stablemen took care of the horses (there might be more than 100 of these). There were keepers for the fishpond and the rabbit warren, which were important sources of food. The miller ground flour from wheat and barley grown on the estate. Gardeners tended the lawns and flowering plants.

Gentleman servants were not usually paid a fixed wage, but were granted areas of farmland instead. They kept the rents and the produce from this land.

Other servants were paid by the year. In the 1560s, a cook earned 10 shillings (50 pence) a year and a farm worker perhaps £1 (equivalent to £700 today). But food and lodgings were free.

HOME COMFORTS

"The floors are strewed with rushes, under which lies an ancient collection of spittle, vomit, dogs' droppings, fishbones and other revolting things", a Dutch visitor wrote in Henry VIII's reign. Early great Tudor houses were smelly, dirty and cold. But by the 1550s they had become cleaner and warmer.

The floors were no longer made of clay or beaten earth. They were paved with stone, or brick tiles, or even with marble. These were much easier to clean. The cold stone walls were covered with tapestries or carved wooden panels.

Fireplaces were made bigger and better. Instead of being out in the centre of the hall, the hearth was now set back into the wall. People began to burn coal instead of wood. This gave out much more heat. The smoke no longer filled the room as it had before, but escaped through channels in the walls and out through tall chimney stacks.

△ **A servant pushes a 'truckle'** (small bed with wheels) back beneath the master's bed. Guests had mattresses filled with goose feathers. Guests' servants slept on truckles or straw mattresses in the galleries or withdrawing chambers.

△ **The lord washes in a basin held by his servant.** Fresh water for the house came through pipes from a nearby spring, or from a well in the courtyard. Some houses had wells in their kitchens. Few people drank water. They preferred beer.

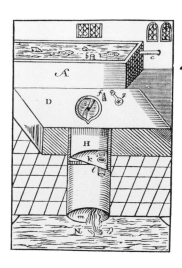

◁ **The lord of the house being dressed by his servants.** His clothes are kept in a chest. He is going out hunting, and is about to put on a short cloak that will not get in his way. The cloak is lined with fur. Some cloaks were embroidered with gold.

◁ **Four men play a game of cards for money.** In Tudor times, card playing was very popular. (Modern card packs still show the King, Queen and Jack in Tudor dress.) People played other indoor games like this after dinner, including chess and shove ha'penny. Billiards was introduced in Elizabeth I's time.

There were very few chairs in early Tudor times. Wolsey's Hampton Court had 280 beds, but only five grand chairs. Most people sat on stools or benches. By Elizabeth I's reign, chairs were more common, especially in great houses. They were ornately carved, and covered with cushions of velvet or silk cloth.

Medieval tables were simple boards laid on trestles. Now, rich families dined at vast and heavy tables made of oak or elm, with thick carved legs. The tables were often covered with carpets (which were not yet put on the floors). Beside the table stood the wooden cupboard, also carved with elaborate patterns.

△ **A coffer**, or chest, that was used to store papers when the owner was travelling. It is covered with leather decorated with gold. In front of the coffer are Tudor writing tools – a 'quill' pen (a bird's feather sharpened at the tip), an ink-pot and writing paper. Documents were hand-written.

△ **Workmen plaster the ceiling of a great chamber.** Owners rarely stopped improving their houses with new decoration and building.

△ **Diagram of the water closet**, invented by Sir John Harington in 1596. The flush lavatory was not widely used until about 1700. Until then, people used chamber pots or the 'privy', a tiny room which might have a seat over a shaft leading to the drains.

◁ **Hardwick Hall in Derbyshire**, with its hundreds of glass window panes.

THE GARDENS

Elizabethan explorers brought hundreds of exotic plants into Britain. The owners of vast new gardens were delighted. "There is not almost one nobleman that hath not a great store of these flowers", wrote the traveller William Harrison in 1577.

Lilacs came from Persia, sunflowers from Peru, tulips from Turkey and marigolds from Africa. These, and old favourites like roses and violets, made gardens more colourful than ever before.

But everything in a Tudor garden had to be neat and regular, to show that the owner could create order out of the wilderness of nature. The gardens had square sides lined with tidy hedges or walls. Straight paths ran between them. The paths, terraces and flower beds were laid out in careful patterns. Statues and pieces of topiary (trees trimmed into animal or bird shapes) stood at intervals.

▷ **A nobleman and his wife** stroll through their knot garden. This was a fashionable kind of planting in Elizabethan times. The outlines of the 'knot' are made of clipped low hedges of herbs and shrubs, which seem to weave in and out of each other. The spaces in between are filled with gravel, sand and flowers. In the corner of the garden is a stone summer house (based on Montacute in Somerset).

▷ **Damask roses did not just look pretty.** The sweet-smelling petals were dried and placed in bowls about the house, or soaked to make rose-water, which was used as a scent and in cooking.

△ **The title page of a herbal**, a gardening book printed in 1597. Most of the plants listed had medicinal properties.

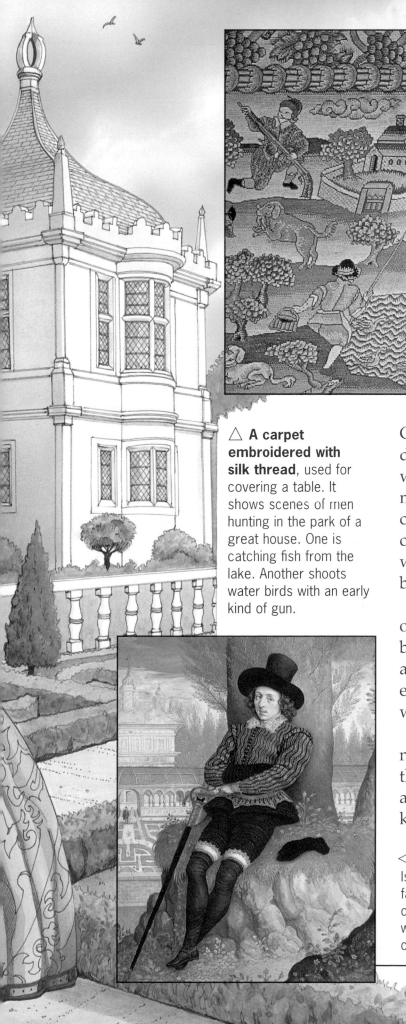

△ **A carpet embroidered with silk thread**, used for covering a table. It shows scenes of men hunting in the park of a great house. One is catching fish from the lake. Another shoots water birds with an early kind of gun.

Great gardens, like great houses, were designed to impress people. Some had wide gravel paths, and perhaps huge marble fountains. Others had rills, or channels of running water, filled with coloured pebbles. At Theobalds the rills were large enough for rowing boats to be used in them.

Most impressive of all were the mazes, or labyrinths. These were winding paths between high hedges, with dead ends and false turnings, where people could easily get lost. Two of the biggest mazes were at Longleat and Hampton Court.

The kitchen garden was also laid out neatly. It was protected from winds by thick hedges or walls. Fruit, vegetables and herbs grown here were taken to the kitchens for cooking.

◁ **A young man seated under a tree**, painted by Isaac Oliver in about 1590. The man, dressed in fashionable clothes, is sitting on a raised area overlooking a grand garden. You can see the garden wall and the neatly shaped beds. Beyond them is a covered walkway made of carved stone.

IN THE KITCHENS

In 1577, the queen spent five days at Sir Nicholas Bacon's great house. She and her court ate 60 sheep, 8 oxen, 18 calves, 34 lambs, over 600 chickens and huge numbers of other birds, including herons, pheasants, quails and larks. Sir Nicholas had to hire twelve extra cooks from London to prepare all this!

▽ **The salt cellar was put on the top table**, where special guests sat. Other tables were 'below the salt'.

◁ **Gardeners raking and digging in a kitchen garden.** Vegetables were rarely eaten with meat, but served on their own as a cooked salad. Potatoes, brought from South America, did not become widely popular until the 1600s.

18

The Elizabethan nobleman ate and drank a lot. Breakfast was a simple meal, but a hearty one if the nobleman was going hunting afterwards. During Henry VIII's reign, the Earl of Northumberland usually had for breakfast a loaf of bread with fish or beef, which he washed down with a litre of beer.

Dinner was served in the middle of the day. The meal started at about eleven o'clock, and might last until three o'clock in the afternoon. The main dishes were meat – mutton and beef, followed by chickens or game, with plenty of bread. At the end of the meal came fruit and biscuits.

On ordinary days, supper was a light meal eaten at about five o'clock. But when there was an important guest, evening was the time to hold a grand feast. When Henry VIII held a banquet for a visiting emperor in 1517, there were ten courses and the meal lasted for seven hours!

▽ **Round wooden mats**, with painted flowers and rhymes. Sweet 'desserts', such as sugared fruits, jellies, spiced cakes and marzipan, were eaten off the plain side.

◁ **A hectic scene** as a huge feast is prepared in the main kitchens of a great house. Can you spot
● The chief cook, finishing preparing a stuffed swan.
● The kitchen boy, helping to turn the spit on which a pig is roasting.
● The scullery man, hanging up game birds, a rabbit and a hare.
● The cellarer, bringing up wine from the cellar.
● The grooms, carrying dishes of cooked food?

◁ **The old kitchen at Burghley House.** Polished pans of copper and iron hang round the walls. At the back is the fireplace. In Tudor times this would have been open, with the fire on the stone hearth. Pots for boiling food were placed on stands above the fire, or hung from hooks.

◁ **A line of waiters** sets off for the great chamber. The nobleman had his own carver and server. The king or queen had 'beefeaters' who first tested that meat was safe for the monarch to eat.

The kitchens of a great house were usually on the ground floor, or even in the basement. The waiters had to carry the dishes up one or two flights of stairs. By the time it reached the table, the food must have grown cold.

Next to the main kitchen were the scullery (where plates and pans were washed) and the larder (where food was stored).

THE QUEEN ARRIVES

Elizabeth I went on her summer progresses for three main reasons. One was to avoid the risk of disease in London. The second was to give people the chance to see their ruler. The third was to save money: her hosts paid for all her food and entertainment.

Acting as host to the queen and her court was certainly expensive. She usually arrived with a staff of more than 1,000 people, plus well over 2,000 horses. (A list of the monarch's travelling staff contained thirty different jobs, the majority of which were done by men.) All the staff and horses had to be fed, and given shelter and bedding.

Sir Christopher Hatton built a vast house at Holdenby in Northamptonshire simply because he hoped that Elizabeth would stay there. It cost so much that he got badly into debt – and the queen never did come to stay. But she stayed with Lord Burghley thirteen times, and each visit cost him nearly £3,000 (over £2 million in today's money).

▷ **Elizabeth waves to a crowd of her subjects** as she passes on a progress in her ornate litter. The carved figure blowing the trumpet is a symbol of Fame.

△ **The Great Pond at Elvetham in Hampshire.** This was specially dug for the queen's visit in 1591, and a pageant was staged on the islands. Elizabeth is sitting on the left.

▷ **Crowds gather excitedly** to watch the queen arriving in the courtyard of a great house, followed by her baggage train. This was made up of more than 400 wagons that carried her clothes, jewellery and furniture. Nobles and grooms rush to greet the queen.

Everything was done to impress the queen. Some noblemen gave her expensive presents, such as beautiful clothes or fans set with diamonds. Others put on lavish shows to amuse her. When she visited the Earl of Leicester at Kenilworth Castle in 1575, she was entertained for three weeks. Among other things there were fireworks, concerts and acrobatic displays. One play was performed on the lake, starring a giant mermaid and a dolphin-like monster.

Why did the owners of palaces and great houses go to such trouble and expense? Most noblemen wanted to impress the queen because she gave important jobs or honours to those who pleased her.

▽ **Elizabeth at a picnic** in the park of a great house. She has spent the morning hunting. The huntsmen carry hunting horns.

SURVIVORS

In medieval times, castles and cathedrals were the greatest and most beautiful buildings in Britain. But in the Tudor Age castles were no longer needed, and there were enough cathedrals and churches. People spent their money building great houses instead.

▽ **A picture of the wedding feast of Sir Henry Unton**, painted after his death in 1596. The feast is probably taking place in his great chamber.

Many of these wonderful Tudor houses can still be seen today. They have been changed and developed over the years, and modern comforts like electricity and running water have been added. But most of the original features are still there. The Great Hall at Longleat, the Long Gallery at Hardwick Hall and the kitchens and gardens at Hampton Court all give a vivid idea of how wealthy people lived in the sixteenth century.

But several of the great houses have sadly vanished for ever. Henry VIII's huge Nonsuch Palace was pulled down in 1682, simply so that the bricks and timber could be sold. The site of Lord Burghley's great mansion, Theobalds, is empty. Others, such as Sir Christopher Hatton's Holdenby, stand in ruins.

◁ **Little Moreton Hall in Cheshire**, built of timber and plasterwork which makes a complex black and white pattern. It was begun in the 15th century, but extended during Elizabeth's reign.

△ **Sir Henry and his guests** are watching a masque, or short play. The actors, dressed as cherubs or women with red-painted faces, walk round an orchestra of six musicians.

GLOSSARY

buttery the room in a large house where butts, or barrels, of ale and preserved meat were kept. (The name has nothing to do with butter.)

chaplain the clergyman who conducted religious services.

civil war a war fought between groups of people in the same country.

ewery the jugs and plates belonging to a nobleman.

game wild animals hunted and killed for their meat.

gentleman a person born into an important family.

groom a servant.

litter a couch with shafts, usually carried by people or horses.

manor an estate with family house and fields.

mason a craftsman who builds with stone.

masque a short play in verse with music.

master craftsman a skilled worker who often teaches others his trade.

moat a ditch filled with water set as a defence around a house.

monastery a community of monks who live according to religious vows.

mutton the meat from a fully-grown sheep.

pageant a series of scenes telling the story of some historical event.

pewter a metal made by mixing tin with copper and lead.

progress a journey made by a king or queen through their country.

smith a metalworker making objects of iron.

steward the head of the staff in a great house.

taffeta a kind of silk cloth.

tapestry a heavy sheet of cloth woven with pictures or patterns for hanging on the wall.

yeoman a servant from the class of farmers who owned land.

▷ **Important Tudor houses and palaces in Britain,** many of which have survived to the present day. The map includes those places listed on page 2.

TIMECHART

1485 Henry Tudor, a Welshman, becomes King Henry VII of England. The Tudor Age lasted from 1485 to 1603.

1501 Richmond Palace completed.

1509 Henry VIII becomes king.

1511 Building begins of Thornbury Castle, the last great fortress (never finished).

1514 Wolsey begins Hampton Court.

1534 The English Reformation: Henry closes down monasteries.

1538 Nonsuch Palace built.

1547 Death of Henry VIII. Edward VI is king.

1553 Mary I becomes queen.

1558 Elizabeth I becomes queen. Start of the 'Elizabethan' period.

1564 Burghley begins to build Theobalds.

1567 Sir John Thynne begins Longleat House.

1580 Building of Crichton Castle begins in Scotland.

1589 Burghley House built.

1591 Building of Hardwick Hall begins.

1603 Death of Queen Elizabeth I.

INDEX